THE BEST LITTLE
GRILLING
COOKBOOK

by Karen Adler

CELESTIALARTS
Berkeley, California

Special thanks to
Mary Ann Duckers, Judith Fertig, Jean Tamburello,
and Shifra Stein
for their contributions to this book.

CELESTIAL ARTS

P.O. Box 7123
Berkeley, CA 94707

Printed in Singapore.

Cover design: Catherine Jacobes
Cover art: Paul Keppel
Interior illustrations: Barry's Clip Art, Basting brush by Brad Greene
Text design: Greene Design

Library of Congress Catalog Card Number: 00-131235

Other cookbooks in this series:
Best Little Barbecue Cookbook
Best Little Marinades Cookbook
Best Little BBQ Sauces Cookbook

Celestial Arts titles are distributed in Canada by Ten Speed Canada, in the
United Kingdom and Europe by Airlift Books, in South Africa by Real Books,
in Australia by Simon & Schuster Australia, in New Zealand by Southern
Publishers Group, and in Southeast Asia by Berkeley Books.

Introduction

Grilling is a summer ritual that has become a year-round passion for many Americans. Outdoor grillers who live in parts of the country with milder climates find themselves no longer waiting for Memorial Day to fire up their barbecues. And with the convenience of gas grills that only require the turn of a knob, it's never been easier to grill your favorite meat, poultry, wild game, vegetables, and even pizza!

Indoor grills and outdoor kitchens have also had an impact on the grilling market. With such fancy equipment, home cooks want to know the secrets to wonderfully grilled foods. A variety of recipes for every kind of cook can be found on these small pages. They are accompanied by savory rubs, marinades, and sauces. So strap on your tongs and let your taste buds have their way!

GRILLING BASICS

Grilling is a fast method of cooking over a direct heat source. Because the intense heat chars or browns the outside of the food, food needs to be turned while grilling for even cooking. Grilling is suited to foods that are tender and require short cooking times—like steaks and burgers.

Grills come in a variety of shapes and sizes with several fuel choices. For gas or electric grills, it is important to read the manufacturer's instructions for best results. The same goes for charcoal grills.

Determining the grill temperature is easy. If you can hold your hand 5 inches above the heat source for 2 seconds, your fire is hot; 3 to 4 seconds is a medium-hot fire, and 5 to 6 seconds is a low fire.

GRILL TIPS:

- ◆ To start a charcoal fire, use a charcoal chimney. Place 15 pieces of lump charcoal in the top of the chimney. Put crumpled paper in the bottom and place on top of your grill. Light the paper; the coals will be white hot in about 15 minutes. Grill over ashen coals that are very hot for best results.
- ◆ Apply nonstick cooking spray to lightly oil the grill grates to help prevent sticking before you light the fire.

- Add a little oil to your marinades or lightly coat the food you plan to grill with some olive oil to help prevent sticking on the grill grates.
- Stiff wire brushes with a scraper make cleaning the grill a simple job (tackle this while the grill is still warm).
- Grill racks are grates to place on top of your grill to accommodate smaller and more delicate items like vegetables, shrimp, and fish, so that they don't fall through the regular grill grates.
- Grill woks are handy for placing on top of the grill and cooking a medley of small chopped meats and vegetables similar to stir-fry, only we call it stir-grill.
- Kabob baskets are time-savers. Instead of threading cubed foods onto skewers, just cut your food into chunks, drop them into the basket, and you're ready to grill in a snap.
- Fresh herbs can be soaked in water and thrown onto your hot barbecue fire to create a lovely aroma in your backyard. Try placing long-stemmed herbs on the grill rack and then cooking fish atop the herbs.
- Create an herb-basting brush by tying herbs together with florist wire. Then dip into a flavored oil and apply to the food that you are grilling.
- Dried herbs can also be soaked in water, then tossed onto the barbecue fire for an aromatic scent.
- Long-handled utensils help to keep your hands and arms at a distance from the fire.

- ◆ Mitts are also helpful to avoid too much heat to your hands.
- ◆ Spray bottles filled with either water or fruit juices do double duty by dousing any unwanted flames and keeping the meat that you are grilling moist.
- ◆ A meat thermometer makes guesswork unnecessary. Digital meat thermometers are excellent for grilling because they gauge the temperature immediately.
- ◆ Wood choices for grilling are wood chips that need to be water-soaked for 30 minutes prior to use. Popular flavors include apple, cherry, grape, oak, alder, hickory, mesquite, pecan, and woody herbs.
- ◆ Keep an assortment of nonperishable condiments in your pantry for creating quick marinades, sauces, glazes, and rubs, including assorted oils and vinegars; a variety of mustards, ketchup, barbecue sauce, Italian salad dressing, soy sauce, Worcestershire sauce, hot sauce, jams or jellies; assorted seasoned salts and peppers, chili powder, paprika, cumin, coriander; and assorted dried herbs like parsley, oregano, basil, rosemary, thyme, and tarragon.
- ◆ Fresh ingredients that enhance foods on the grill include garlic, onions, peppers, citrus, and fresh herbs.

GRILLING RECIPES

Grilled Catfish Fillets with Aioli

Farm-raised catfish are firmer and milder than their wild counterparts. Thus, they are better suited to the grill and are enhanced with flavorful relishes and sauces.

6 farm-raised catfish fillets
1 to 2 teaspoons olive oil
1/2 teaspoon white pepper
1/2 teaspoon seasoned black pepper
1/2 teaspoon garlic salt

AIOLI:
2 egg yolks
1 cup olive oil
1 tablespoon lemon juice
2 anchovy fillets, minced
2 cloves garlic, minced
2 teaspoons fresh basil (or 1 teaspoon dried)
1/2 teaspoon Worcestershire sauce

¹/₂ teaspoon red wine vinegar
Salt and Tabasco to taste

To make aioli, place egg yolks in a medium-sized glass bowl and microwave for 15 to 20 seconds. Whisk egg yolks together and slowly drizzle in the olive oil. If mixture gets too thick, add lemon juice and thin with a little warm water. Add the garlic, basil, salt, Tabasco, Worcestershire, vinegar, and anchovies. Mix thoroughly and chill.

Makes about 1 cup

Prepare and preheat the grill. Lightly coat the catfish fillets with olive oil, then sprinkle with peppers and garlic salt. Place on top of a greased grill rack and place rack over hot coals. Grill for 10 minutes per inch of thickness, turning once, until fish flakes easily. Serve with a dollop of aioli.

Serves 6

GRILLING

HALIBUT FILLET WITH RED PEPPER BEURRE BLANC

Halibut is an exceptional medium-firm fish for the grill. Try grilling a whole fillet for beautiful presentation. For best results, buy fish with the skin intact, because it helps to keep it from falling apart on the grill.

4 to 6 halibut fillets, 7 to 8 ounces each

1 to 2 tablespoons olive oil

RED PEPPER BEURRE BLANC:

1/2 cup white wine

1 tablespoon tarragon vinegar

1 medium red bell pepper, chopped

1 shallot, diced

1/4 cup heavy cream

1/2 cup (1 stick) unsalted butter, chilled

Salt to taste

In a saucepan, combine the wine, vinegar, shallot, and red pepper. Bring to a slow boil and reduce until 2 tablespoons of liquid remain. Add cream and boil 2 minutes. Lower heat and whisk in butter a little at a time, until all butter is incorporated. Remove from heat and place sauce in a blender on medium speed for 1 minute. Strain, then season with salt. Set aside.

Prepare and preheat the grill. Brush fillets with olive oil and grill flesh side down over hot coals for 4 to 5 minutes. Then turn to the skin side and grill for 4 to 5 minutes more. Flesh will get milky and opaque. Serve with beurre blanc spooned over fillets.

Serves 4

GRILLING   **13**

Pistachio-Buttered Mahi Mahi

Pistachio butter is deliciously versatile and marries well with poultry and pork or substitute trout, walleye, or whitefish for the mahi mahi.

8 (4-ounce) mahi mahi fillets
3/4 cup vegetable oil
Salt and freshly ground pepper to taste

PISTACHIO BUTTER:
1/2 cup (1 stick) butter, softened
1/4 cup finely chopped pistachios

Prepare and preheat the grill. Coat fish fillets with oil and season with salt and pepper. Set aside.

In a small bowl, combine softened butter and nuts. Spoon into a ramekin or small bowl.

Grill fillets on a greased grill topper over hot coals for 5 minutes per side. Serve 2 fillets per person and top with a pat of pistachio butter.

Serves 4

CITRUS STIR-GRILLED SCALLOPS AND SHRIMP

For a colorful presentation, serve the skewers on a bed of thinly sliced oranges and cucumbers. If using bamboo skewers, be sure to soak them in water before using so they won't burn on the grill.

1/2 pound scallops
1/2 pound large shrimp, shelled and deveined
Grated zest of 1 lemon
Juice of 1 lemon
Juice of 1 lime
Juice of 1/2 orange
3 tablespoons orange liqueur

Combine all ingredients in a bowl and marinate for 1 to 2 hours in the refrigerator. Remove seafood and reserve the liquid for basting.

Prepare and preheat the grill. Thread scallops and shrimp alternately onto 4 skewers. Grill, basting frequently with reserved marinade until just cooked, 6 to 8 minutes.

Serves 2

STIR-GRILLED SALMON WITH SUGAR SNAP PEAS

This is my favorite grill wok recipe. It combines texture, color, and taste at its best. For a smokey flavor, add a handful of water-soaked alder chips to the hot coals while grilling.

1 pound salmon steak or fillets, cut into cubes

1/2 pound sugar snap peas, stems removed

12 cherry tomatoes

1/2 red onion, sliced

3 cups cooked white rice

MARINADE:

1/4 cup soy sauce

1/4 cup rice wine vinegar

2 tablespoons honey

4 cloves garlic, minced

1 teaspoon ginger

1 teaspoon sesame paste

 Combine marinade ingredients in a large glass bowl. Add salmon cubes and peas to marinade with tomatoes and onions. Marinate for about 30 minutes.

Prepare and preheat the grill. Pour salmon mixture into a well-greased grill wok over the sink and partially drain liquid. Place wok over hot coals and stir-grill fish and vegetables, tossing with large wooden spoons for 6 to 8 minutes. Move wok to indirect-heat side of grill. Close lid on grill and cook for another 4 to 5 minutes. Serve with rice.

Serves 4

GRILLED SWORDFISH WITH MANGO RELISH AND LEMON GRASS ESSENCE

Lemon grass has a vibrant lemon flavor. If it is not available, try substituting lemon zest, lemon balm, or lemon verbena for similar results.

MANGO RELISH:

2 mangoes, diced small

1/3 cup finely chopped fresh cilantro

1 shallot, finely diced

1/2 teaspoon grated fresh ginger

Juice of 1 lime

Combine all ingredients and store tightly covered in refrigerator until ready to use.

LEMON GRASS ESSENCE:

2 tablespoons dry white wine

1 shallot, chopped

1 teaspoon finely chopped lemon grass

2/3 cup unsalted butter, cut into cubes

In saucepan, heat wine, shallot, and lemon grass over medium-low heat and reduce liquid by two-thirds. Add butter, a cube at a time, and mix well. Strain and season to taste.

8 portions center-cut swordfish, 7 ounces each
1/2 cup apple wood chips, water-soaked
Pink peppercorns

Prepare and preheat the grill. Grill swordfish over hot coals with moistened apple chips added until done, about 4 to 5 minutes per side. Spoon Mango Relish onto each dinner plate.

To serve, place swordfish in the center of each plate, pour Lemon Grass Essence on the fish and around the rest of the plate, and garnish with pink peppercorns.

Serves 8

GRILLING

TUNA WITH QUICK ROUILLE

Rouille is a rust-colored sauce used primarily in Mediterranean fish soups and stews. It is delicious served with grilled fish. It is also a great dipping sauce with grilled vegetables.

4 tuna steaks, 6 to 8 ounces each

4 tablespoons pink peppercorns

4 tablespoons green peppercorns

1 lemon, cut into wedges

QUICK ROUILLE:

1 cup good-quality mayonnaise

6 cloves garlic, minced

1 tablespoon lemon juice

1/2 teaspoon salt

1/4 teaspoon saffron threads

1/4 teaspoon cayenne pepper

To make rouille, in a food processor combine mayonnaise, lemon juice, garlic, and salt. Pulse on and off for 1 to 2 minutes. Transfer to a bowl and stir in the saffron and pepper to blend. Keeps refrigerated for about 2 days.

Makes 1 cup

Prepare and preheat the grill. Crush together pink and green peppercorns and coat surface of each steak. Grill fish over a hot fire for approximately 2½ minutes per side. (Notice the short cooking time: tuna will toughen if overcooked.) Serve with lemon wedges and a dollop of rouille.

Serves 4

Chilled Grilled Shrimp with Tomato Salsa

This makes a lovely cool appetizer or try serving over dressed mixed greens for a refreshing main course salad.

1 pound shrimp, peeled and deveined
1 cup peanut oil
3 cloves fresh garlic, minced
1/4 cup lemon juice
1 teaspoon seasoned salt
1/4 teaspoon dried thyme
1/4 teaspoon dried basil
1/4 teaspoon dried oregano

TOMATO SALSA:

2 cups prepared salsa
1 tomato, chopped
1 teaspoon lime juice
1 tablespoon chopped fresh cilantro
1/2 teaspoon freshly ground black pepper

Combine the tomato salsa ingredients, mix well, and chill.

In a medium bowl, combine all of the shrimp ingredients. Cover and refrigerate for about 8 hours.

Prepare and preheat grill wok. Drain off marinade and grill shrimp in grill wok over a hot fire for approximately 6 minutes or until just cooked through. Spread out cooked shrimp and cool completely. May be refrigerated overnight. Serve with Tomato Salsa.

Serves 4

HONEY-MUSTARD TURKEY TENDERS

Serve this with grilled sweet potatoes.

4 bacon-wrapped turkey tenderloins
1/4 cup country-style German mustard
2 tablespoons honey
2 tablespoons firmly packed dark brown sugar
1 tablespoon balsamic vinegar
1/2 teaspoon sesame oil

Combine mustard, honey, brown sugar, vinegar, and sesame oil in a glass bowl.

Place tenderloins in a sealable plastic bag and pour marinade over turkey. Seal the bag and refrigerate several hours or overnight.

Prepare and preheat the grill. Remove the turkey from marinade and grill over hot fire for 10 to 12 minutes, turning turkey every 3 minutes.

Serves 4

ASIAN GRILLED CHICKEN

Serve this with a cold Chinese noodle salad.

1 chicken fryer, cut up, 2 to 3 pounds
1/4 cup soy sauce
2 tablespoons rice vinegar
2 tablespoons lemon juice
1/2 teaspoon Tabasco sauce
2 green onions, finely chopped
1 clove garlic, crushed

Rinse chicken and place in a large sealable plastic bag. Combine marinade ingredients and pour into bag with chicken. Marinate for 6-8 hours in the refrigerator.

Prepare and preheat the grill. Remove chicken from the marinade and grill over a medium-hot fire for 20 to 30 minutes, turning occasionally until done. Cover grill with lid to increase heat for faster cooking.

Serves 4

Chicken Legs with Herbed Goat Cheese Stuffing

The herbed goat cheese mixture is a savory spread on toasted French bread garnished with fresh relish of chopped garden tomatoes and scallions.

4 tablespoons goat cheese

1 clove garlic, crushed

3 tablespoons chopped fresh herbs, such as chives, oregano, or parsley

2 tablespoons fresh brown bread crumbs

Salt and freshly ground black pepper

8 chicken drumsticks

8 slices hickory-smoked bacon

1 tablespoon olive oil

1 teaspoon Grey Poupon mustard

In a bowl, combine the goat cheese, garlic, herbs, and bread crumbs. Season with salt and pepper to taste. Carefully loosen the skin from each drumstick. Spoon goat cheese mixture under the skin. Tightly wrap a bacon slice around each drumstick to hold the skin and stuffing in place during cooking. Combine the mustard and oil and brush them over the chicken.

Prepare and preheat the grill. Cook legs on a medium-hot grill for about 25 minutes, turning and basting occasionally.

Serves 4

ALL-AMERICAN GRILLED CHICKEN SALAD

Add a little fresh chopped tarragon, cured olives, and lemon zest or juice for a continental twist.

4 chicken breast fillets

1 tablespoon olive oil

Salt and pepper to taste

1 stalk celery, diced

1/2 teaspoon seasoned salt

1/4 teaspoon black pepper

1/4 cup mayonnaise

Lettuce leaves

Tomato slices

Hard-boiled eggs, halved

Black and green olives

Broccoli florets

 Prepare and preheat grill.

Rinse chicken and pat dry. Coat with oil and season with salt and pepper. Grill over hot fire for about 15 minutes, turning once. Remove from the grill, cool and dice. In a large bowl, combine chicken with celery, seasonings, and mayonnaise, and mix well. Chill. Serve on a bed of lettuce with tomato slices, hard-boiled eggs, olives, and broccoli florets.

Serves 8

GRILLED SPICY LEMON CHICKEN WINGS

For a smokey Southwest flavor, add a handful of water-soaked mesquite chips to your hot fire.

2 pounds chicken wings, jointed, tips removed
Juice of 2 lemons
1 cup Italian dressing
3 tablespoons butter, melted

Combine the Italian dressing, lemon juice, and melted butter. Marinate chicken in a bowl or a sealable plastic bag in the refrigerator for at least 20 minutes or up to 2 hours.

Prepare and preheat the grill. Grill chicken wings over medium to hot coals, basting with marinade mixture every 5 minutes. Grill for about 20 minutes.

Serves 4

Moroccan-Style Grilled Chicken

This versatile recipe makes a delicious salad too.

4 chicken breast fillets
1 cup olive oil
1/2 cup lemon juice
1/4 cup chopped fresh parsley
2 cloves garlic, crushed
1 teaspoon ground cumin
Salt and freshly ground pepper to taste
2 cups cooked couscous

Combine olive oil, lemon juice, parsley, garlic, cumin, and salt and pepper. Place chicken in a sealable plastic bag and pour 1/2 the marinade into bag and seal. Marinate for 1 hour in the refrigerator.

Prepare and preheat the grill. Remove chicken from marinade and grill over hot fire for about 12 to 15 minutes, turning once. Serve with hot couscous drizzled with reserved marinade.

Serves 4

GRILLING

Spaghettini Napoletana with Parmesan Grilled Chicken

Grill extra chicken one day, then prepare this recipe the next day with the leftover chicken for a time-saving step.

4 chicken breast fillets
1 tablespoon olive oil
4 tablespoons freshly grated Parmesan cheese
2 tablespoons toasted bread crumbs
Salt and freshly ground pepper to taste

SPAGHETTINI NAPOLETANA:

16 ounces spaghettini, cooked until al dente,
   then drained
1/3 cup olive oil
4 whole cloves garlic
4 cups chopped canned Roma tomatoes
4 tablespoons chopped fresh basil
4 tablespoons minced garlic
Salt and pepper to taste
4 tablespoons grated Romano cheese

Prepare and preheat the grill. Rinse chicken well and pat dry. Coat chicken with 1 tablespoon oil, cheese, bread crumbs, salt, and pepper. Grill over hot fire for about 5 to 6 minutes per side. Remove from grill and keep warm.

Heat $1/3$ cup oil in a large sauté pan. Add garlic cloves and brown slightly, then add tomatoes. Simmer, stirring occasionally. Add basil, minced garlic, salt, and pepper. Cook for approximately 10 to 15 minutes, stirring occasionally. Reheat cooked pasta in hot water, drain well, and add to the tomatoes, tossing to combine. Add Romano cheese and mix well. Serve at once topped with a golden chicken breast.

Serves 4

Grilled Chicken with Pesto

Pesto is Italian and its French counterpart, pistou, is similarly prepared, but without the pine nuts and cheese. Try it for a change.

4 chicken breast fillets

Juice of l lemon

Freshly ground pepper to taste

2 tablespoons olive oil

Sliced tomatoes

PESTO:

2 cups torn, fresh basil leaves

$1/2$ cup pine nuts

l clove garlic, crushed

$1/2$ cup grated Parmesan cheese

$3/4$ cup olive oil

34

In a food processor purée the basil leaves, pine nuts, garlic, and 1/4 cup Parmesan cheese. Gradually add oil and remaining cheese. Refrigerate, then bring to room temperature before serving.

Prepare and preheat the grill. Drizzle lemon juice over chicken and season with pepper. Let stand for 15 minutes. Lightly brush with olive oil and grill over hot coals for about 5 minutes per side, until done. Serve with pesto and sliced tomatoes.

Serves 4

GRILLED ASPARAGUS

Add a handful of water-soaked oak chips to the hot fire for a fragrant smokey flavor.

1 pound fresh asparagus, trimmed

1/4 cup teriyaki sauce

2 tablespoons vinegar

4 cloves garlic, minced

1 teaspoon dried ginger

1 teaspoon toasted sesame oil

2 teaspoons toasted sesame seeds for garnish

 Arrange asparagus spears on a baking tray. In a small bowl, combine the rest of the ingredients (reserving sesame seeds for garnish). Brush half the marinade over the asparagus.

Prepare and preheat the grill. Grease a grill basket or rack and grill asparagus until crisp-tender and slightly charred. Drizzle remaining marinade over hot asparagus. Garnish with sesame seeds.

Serves 4

GRILLING

TANDOORI GRILLED CHICKEN

This yogurt and Indian spice marinade keeps chicken moist and flavorful. This versatile recipe can be used on tuna steaks, skewered shrimp or scallops, and cod or haddock.

8 chicken breast fillets

1 cup yogurt

4 or 5 cloves garlic, minced

1 teaspoon grated fresh ginger

1 teaspoon cayenne pepper

2 teaspoons ground cumin

2 teaspoons ground coriander

1 teaspoon salt

4 tablespoons vegetable oil

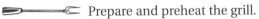 Prepare and preheat the grill.

Rinse chicken and set aside. Combine all of the marinade ingredients in a large glass bowl and blend well. Add chicken and marinate for 30 minutes. Remove chicken from marinade and grill over a hot fire for about 12 to 15 minutes, turning once, until golden brown and firm to touch.

Serves 8

Garden Vegetable Stir-Grill

Homemade vinaigrette is so easy to make.
Use half for the vegetables and the other half
for a mixed green salad.

1 pint cherry tomatoes, whole
2 small zucchini, sliced
2 small yellow squash, sliced
1 red onion, sliced
1 bell pepper (green, red, or yellow), sliced
1/2 cup Italian dressing

 Rinse and prepare vegetables. Place in a large bowl, add salad dressing, and marinate for 1/2 hour.

Prepare and preheat the grill. Pour mixture into a greased grill basket over the sink (to drain dressing). Grill for about 10 to 12 minutes over a hot fire, tossing several times, then serve immediately. Vegetables will be crisp-tender.

Serves 8

Romano-Grilled Broccoli

A grill wok or grill basket is an easy way to prepare a dish like this. The wok keeps the small florets from falling through the large grill grates.

l large bunch broccoli, preferably garden-fresh

3 tablespoons extra-virgin olive oil

2 large cloves garlic, minced

1/2 cup freshly grated Romano cheese

5 fresh basil leaves, torn in pieces

Prepare and preheat the grill.

Trim broccoli stalks, remove leaves, and peel stalks with a vegetable peeler, cutting crosswise into quarter inch slices. Break florets into large bite-size pieces and toss with the olive oil and minced garlic. Place broccoli in a greased grill wok and cook over a hot fire. Grill for about 12 minutes, tossing several times while cooking. Garnish with the cheese and basil and serve.

Serves 4

GRILLED GARDEN ONIONS

This recipe is courtesy of Shifra Stein, author of Vegetables on the Grill *(1998, Pig Out Publications).*

4 medium-large garden onions
1/3 cup olive oil
1 tablespoon balsamic vinegar
1 tablespoon minced fresh tarragon
Salt and freshly ground pepper to taste
2 teaspoons unsalted butter

Prepare and preheat the grill.
Cut tops and bottoms of each onion and peel. Combine oil, vinegar, tarragon, and seasonings. Coat onions thoroughly with mixture. Place 1/2 teaspoon of butter on top of each onion, and then wrap each onion tightly in foil. Place directly on the coals over high heat until tender, brown, and sizzling hot about 20 to 30 minutes. Remove from foil and serve.

Serves 4

GRILLED PORTOBELLO MUSHROOM "BURGER"

An herbed mayonnaise or spicy mustard are very tasty sauces to serve as condiments with this haute-cuisine burger!

4 large portobello mushrooms

2 tablespoons olive oil

l clove garlic, peeled and minced

French bread or sesame seed kaiser rolls

Prepare and preheat the grill.

Wash and dry mushrooms. Blend the olive oil and garlic together. Brush on mushrooms. Grill over hot coals about 4 minutes per side. Place mushrooms on bread and serve. Add mayonnaise, lettuce, and tomato, if desired.

Serves 4

STIR-GRILLED SUGAR SNAP AND SNOW PEAS

Make this recipe in the spring or early summer when sugar snap and snow peas are at their peak.

1/2 pound snow peas

1/2 pound sugar snap peas, cleaned and stems removed

12 cherry tomatoes

1/2 red onion, sliced

1/4 cup soy sauce

1/4 cup rice wine vinegar

2 tablespoons honey

4 cloves garlic, minced

1 teaspoon ground ginger

1 teaspoon toasted sesame oil

Combine soy sauce, vinegar, honey, garlic, ginger, and sesame oil in a glass bowl. Add peas, tomatoes, and onions, and marinate for 30 minutes or more. Remove vegetables from marinade and place in a well-greased grill wok. Place wok over a hot fire. Using a large wooden spoon, stir-grill vegetables for 8 to 10 minutes. Spoon extra marinade onto vegetables, being careful of flare-ups. Move wok to indirect heat side of grill, close lid, and cook for 4 to 5 minutes more.

Serves 4

GRILLING

Parsleyed New Potatoes with Rosemary

Keep the heat out of the kitchen with this recipe that's perfect for placing on the grill while you're cooking some chicken or a steak. Add a salad or fresh tomato slices and dinner is done!

1 1/2 pounds new potatoes, thoroughly
    cleaned

2 tablespoons butter

1/4 cup finely chopped parsley

1 teaspoon fresh rosemary, finely chopped

Salt and pepper to taste

Prepare and preheat the grill.
In a saucepan, cover the potatoes with water and boil for about 10 minutes, or until almost done. Drain and set aside. Tear off a large sheet of aluminum foil. Arrange the potatoes on foil, dot with butter; sprinkle with parsley, rosemary, salt, and pepper. Close up foil package and grill for 10 minutes.

Serves 4

Herb-Grilled Summer Squash

This lovely medley of squash can be served over the pasta of your choice. Another variation is to make a veggie pizza. Spread Dijon mustard on top of a prepared pizza crust. Arrange the grilled summer squash on top and sprinkle with Parmesan cheese. Heat in the oven or on top of the grill until toasty hot.

4 small summer squash (pattypan, zucchini, or crookneck)

2 tablespoons olive oil

1/2 cup chopped fresh herbs (parsley, chives, and/or tarragon)

Salt and freshly ground pepper to taste

Prepare and preheat the grill.

Slice squash about 1 inch thick on the diagonal. Put the squash with the olive oil in a sealable plastic bag and shake to coat. Place squash in a greased grill basket and grill over a hot fire 7 to 10 minutes, tossing every 2 to 3 minutes. The squash are done when they are soft, not mushy. Toss with fresh herbs, salt, and pepper.

Serves 4

GRILLED TOMATOES WITH BLUE CHEESE AND BASIL

Maytag blue cheese is a smooth creamy blue made in Newton, Iowa. You can buy it by mail order: (800) 247-2458.

4 large ripe tomatoes, with top cut off

4 tablespoons crumbled Maytag blue cheese

12 fresh basil leaves (3 leaves per tomato)

 Prepare and preheat the grill. Brush grill rack with oil. Place tomatoes skin-side up on the grill over medium high heat and cook for 5 to 8 minutes, until soft. Turn the tomatoes over, place 1/2 tablespoon blue cheese on each, top with basil leaves, and close grill lid. Cook for another minute or two until cheese is melted.

Serves 4

Skewered Fruit

Grilled fruit does double duty; serve for dessert or as a side with grilled pork, poultry, or seafood.

l large red apple, cut into 8 chunks

2 bananas, cut into 8 chunks

8 chunks of melon

8 chunks of fresh pineapple

¼ cup pineapple juice

Prepare and preheat the grill. Soak 8 bamboo skewers in water for 30 minutes. Alternate fruit among the skewers and brush with pineapple juice. Grill over a hot fire for about 5 to 6 minutes, turning and basting with pineapple juice.

Serves 4

GRILLED FRESH PINEAPPLE COLADA

Homemade coconut ice cream would be worth the extra effort to turn this excellent dessert into the sublime.

l large fresh pineapple, peeled and cored

1 quart pineapple sherbet or sorbet

1 cup shredded toasted coconut

Prepare and preheat the grill. Cut the pineapple into 1-inch-thick rings and place in a grill basket. Grill over medium heat, about 2 minutes per side, until the pineapple has browned and softened.

To serve, place a scoop of pineapple sherbet or sorbet in the center of each grilled pineapple ring. Sprinkle the toasted coconut on top.

Serves 6 to 8

GRILLED PEACHES

Substitute pears or apples or do a medley of fruit on the grill and serve with caramel sauce or a sprinkling of brown sugar.

4 firm peaches

Prepare and preheat the grill. Peel peaches and cut in half (remove the pit). Grill over a medium-hot fire for about 4 minutes per side.

Serves 4

Hickory-Grilled Pork Burger

This recipe is courtesy of Que Queen Jean Tamburello, owner of Marty's Bar-B-Q in Kansas City.

1 pound lean ground pork

3/4 cup finely grated Italian bread crumbs

3/4 cup grated imported Romano cheese

3 eggs

3 cloves fresh garlic, minced

1/3 cup chopped fresh parsley (or 1 tablespoon dried flakes)

1/2 teaspoon salt

1/4 teaspoon black pepper

1 tablespoon chopped fresh basil leaf (or 2 teaspoons dried crushed leaf)

1 package hamburger buns

1 large red onion, sliced

1 large tomato, sliced

4 to 6 lettuce leaves, washed and dried

Marty's Bar-B-Q Sauce (or barbecue sauce of your choice)

In a large bowl, mix with your hands the ground pork, bread crumbs, cheese, eggs, herbs, and spices, and mix thoroughly. Divide into 4 or 5 equal parts. Moisten hands and form into patties approximately 3/4 to 1 inch thick.

Prepare and preheat the grill. Grill burgers over an open flame, with moistened hickory chips added, until meat is well done (patties should not be pink in the middle). Serve on grilled hamburger buns with grilled red onions, fresh sliced tomatoes, lettuce, and barbecue sauce. (Note: patties may be made up in advance and either stored in the refrigerator or frozen for up to 3 months.)

Serves 4

Grilled Pork Chops with Orange-Pineapple Salsa

Complement these succulent pork chops with white rice flecked with green onion.

4 pork chops
Salt and pepper to taste
Cilantro sprigs

ORANGE-PINEAPPLE SALSA:

1/2 fresh pineapple, cored, peeled, and sliced
   into 1-inch pieces
1 Valencia or navel orange, peeled, seeded,
   and diced
1 small red onion, finely chopped
1 shallot, minced
1 clove garlic, minced
1/2 jalapeño pepper, seeded, and diced

¹/₂ cup rice wine

¹/₄ cup firmly packed brown sugar

¹/₄ cup fresh cilantro, chopped

2 tablespoons sherry

Place all Orange-Pineapple Salsa ingredients except cilantro in a large saucepan and simmer over medium-low heat for 20 minutes. Stir frequently. Just before serving, add cilantro and mix.

Prepare and preheat the grill. Grill pork chops over hot coals until medium rare. Spoon some Orange-Pineapple Salsa on each dinner plate and top with a pork chop. Before serving, garnish each with a ribbon of salsa and a cilantro sprig.

Serves 4

Wood-Grilled Pork Loin with Pecan-Sage Sauce

Grilled polenta and sautéed peppers are tasty accompaniments with this pork dish.

1 boneless pork loin, with the fat, about
   1 1/2 pounds
1 to 2 tablespoons chopped fresh sage, or to taste
1 tablespoon minced garlic, or to taste
1 to 2 teaspoons dried thyme, or to taste
Salt and cracked pepper to taste
Pecan wood chips, water-soaked

PECAN-SAGE SAUCE:
1 tablespoon butter
1/2 cup pecan halves
1 teaspoon chopped garlic
1 teaspoon chopped shallot
1/4 cup Madeira wine
2 1/2 cups veal demi-glace or canned beef gravy
1 tablespoon chopped fresh sage
Salt and pepper to taste

Melt butter in a skillet and add pecans, garlic, and shallot. Cook briefly, then add wine. Stir in demi-glace and simmer over medium heat until liquid is thickened and reduced by about one-third. Add sage and adjust seasoning to taste.

Makes about 2 cups

Prepare pork a day ahead. Rub pork with sage, garlic, thyme, salt, and pepper. Place in a sealable plastic bag and refrigerate overnight.

Prepare and preheat the grill. Grill pork loin over hot fire, with moistened pecan chips added, for about 20 to 25 minutes, turning on all sides to char. Cook to not more than 160 degrees F. Spoon warm Pecan-Sage Sauce over pork loin and serve.

Serves 6 to 8

GRILL-RUBBED PORK TENDERLOIN

This grainy rub creates a crisp outer crust on the tenderloin that's very nice.

2 pork tenderloins, 1½ pounds each
1 tablespoon oil

GRILL RUB:

½ cup black pepper
½ cup paprika
¼ cup garlic powder
¼ cup onion powder
3 tablespoons dry mustard
3 tablespoons celery seed
3 tablespoons brown sugar
1 tablespoon sea salt

Combine the rub ingredients. Set 1/2 cup of rub aside and place the rest in a glass jar with tight fitting lid for future use.

In a glass baking dish, coat tenderloins with oil and rub in 1/2 cup of the mix. Cover with plastic wrap and refrigerate for 2 to 3 hours.

Prepare and preheat the grill. Grill tenderloins over hot fire for about 15 to 20 minutes. Let meat stand for 5 minutes, then slice, and serve.

Serves 4 to 6

Hayden Lake Pork Tenderloin with Asian Sauce and Black Sesame Seeds

Arrange the pork on a platter with dipping bowls for the Chinese mustard and the black sesame seeds.

3 pounds boneless pork tenderloin
1 cup Chinese mustard
1 cup black sesame seeds

ASIAN SAUCE:
5 tablespoons hoisin sauce
3 tablespoons plum sauce
2 tablespoons oyster sauce
2 tablespoons soy sauce
2 tablespoons honey
1 tablespoon dry sherry
1 tablespoon peanut oil

¹/₂ teaspoon five-spice powder

1 tablespoon finely minced garlic

1 tablespoon minced fresh ginger

Place tenderloins in a large sealable plastic bag. Blend Asian Sauce ingredients and marinate for 4 to 6 hours or overnight in the refrigerator. Remove pork from marinade. Pour marinade into a small saucepan, bring to a boil, then use as a basting sauce.

Prepare and preheat the grill. Place pork on the grill over a hot fire. Grill for about 20 minutes, turning and brushing occasionally with reserved marinade. Cut in thin slices and serve hot or cold with hot Chinese mustard and black sesame seeds for dipping.

Serves 12 to 15 people as an appetizer

Grilled Pork Tenderloin Salad with Ginger Vinaigrette

Please serve the Ginger Vinaigrette with just about any kind of grilled meat salad.

2 pork tenderloins
Salt and freshly ground black pepper
4 cups mixed greens
3 cups cooked and cooled wild rice

GINGER VINAIGRETTE:
1/4 cup fresh chicken broth
1/4 cup fresh lime juice
3 tablespoons grated fresh ginger
4 green onions, finely chopped
1 tablespoon honey
1 tablespoon soy sauce
1 clove garlic, minced
2 tablespoons olive oil

In a small bowl, whisk together the Ginger Vinaigrette ingredients. Set aside.

Prepare and preheat the grill. Sprinkle pork with salt and pepper. Grill over a hot fire for about 20 minutes.

Toss the mixed greens with half of the Ginger Vinaigrette and arrange on a serving platter. Spoon the wild rice in the center of the greens. Slice the pork tenderloin and arrange on the greens around the rice. Drizzle all with remaining vinaigrette.

Serves 6

Grilled Pork Tenderloin Kabobs

Round out this succulent meat with rice, baked apples, and warm French bread.

2 pork tenderloins, 1½ pounds each, cubed
½ cup Italian dressing
¼ cup soy sauce
1 tablespoon black pepper
1 teaspoon granulated garlic

MUSTARD-HORSERADISH SAUCE:
¾ cup Creole mustard
1 tablespoon pure prepared horseradish
¼ sour cream

Combine Mustard-Horseradish ingredients, blending with a wire whisk. Refrigerate until ready to use.

In a large sealable plastic bag, place cubed pork, dressing, soy sauce, pepper, and garlic. Seal the bag and refrigerate overnight.

Prepare and preheat the grill. Thread pork onto wooden skewers that have been soaked in water for at least 30 minutes. Grill over hot fire for about 8 to 10 minutes, turning meat 2 or 3 times. Serve with Mustard-Horseradish Sauce.

Serves 4

Grilled Ham Slices with Brown Sugar Basting Sauce

The brown sugar baste is excellent with pork chops, tenderloins, steaks, and ribs. Be careful not to apply the baste until the last 5 to 7 minutes of cooking to prevent the sugar from burning.

4 precooked ham slices, each ½ inch thick
Apple wood chips, water-soaked

BROWN SUGAR BASTING SAUCE:
½ cup brown sugar, packed
¼ cup butter, melted
2 tablespoons lemon juice
2 tablespoons dry mustard
2 tablespoons orange zest
1 teaspoon paprika

 Combine the Brown Sugar Basting Sauce ingredients.

Prepare and preheat the grill. Grill ham over medium-hot fire, with moistened apple chips added, for about 2 minutes on each side. Grill and baste with the brown sugar mixture for an additional 5 to 6 minutes turning several times.

Serves 4

Cajun-Style Ribs

Always remove the membrane on the back of the ribs before applying seasonings or marinades. This will make the rib meat easier to pull off the bone while eating.

2 slabs pork baby back ribs, membrane removed

2 tablespoons paprika

2 teaspoons garlic salt

2 teaspoons red pepper

2 teaspoons seasoned black pepper

1 teaspoon chili powder

1 teaspoon thyme

1 teaspoon basil

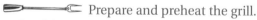 Prepare and preheat the grill.

Combine seasonings and rub all over ribs. Grill ribs over medium-hot fire for about 4 to 5 minutes on each side. Lower heat to medium and place ribs on indirect side of grill. Close lid and cook for 90 minutes until meat shrinks away from end of bones. Wrap in foil and let sit for 1 hour, then cut and serve.

Serves 4

Patio Steaks with Mediterranean Rub

Patio steaks or charcoal steaks are an inexpensive cut from the beef shoulder. They are very tasty, but need to be marinated. Try soaking some rosemary sprigs in water, then adding them to the hot fire while grilling. Your backyard will smell heavenly.

4 patio steaks, each 3/4 inch thick

1 tablespoon olive oil

2 cloves garlic, minced

4 teaspoons dried basil

2 teaspoons freshly ground black pepper

1/4 cup grated Parmesan cheese

Prepare and preheat the grill.

Combine garlic, basil, and pepper and rub each steak liberally with the mixture. Grill the steaks over a hot fire for 5 minutes on each side for medium-rare. Sprinkle with Parmesan cheese.

Serves 4

Papaya Flank Steak with Diablo Sauce

The papaya contains a natural meat tenderizing enzyme called papain; thus the papaya tenderizes the steak and also imparts a delicious fruit flavor.

1 flank steak, 1 or 2 pounds

2 tablespoons sugar

2 tablespoons soy sauce

2 tablespoons black pepper

1 tablespoon kosher salt

1 papaya (or pineapple), peeled and seeded,
    sliced very thin

Sprinkle sugar, soy sauce, pepper, and salt on both sides of steak. Completely cover both sides of steak with the papaya slices. Press meat/fruit combination between two plates. Refrigerate 24 hours.

DIABLO SAUCE:

4 tablespoons butter

1 tablespoon minced garlic

1 tablespoon minced shallot

1/4 cup flour

1/2 teaspoon black pepper

2 teaspoons dry mustard

1 tablespoon Heinz 57 sauce

1 (10-ounce) can beef consommé

In a saucepan, melt butter and sauté garlic and shallots. Add flour and pepper, and cook 2 minutes. In a separate bowl combine dry mustard, Heinz 57 sauce, and consommé and add to flour mixture. Bring to boil, then remove from heat.

Preheat grill to medium-high heat. Cook steak to desired doneness. Slice against the grain at a 45-degree angle. Serve with Diablo Sauce.

Serves 4 to 6

GRILLED RIB-EYE STEAKS

Try this crusty spice mixture on ribs, pork tenderloin, chicken, or even hamburgers.

4 rib-eye steaks, each 1½ inches thick

2 tablespoons vegetable oil

2 tablespoons freshly ground black pepper

2 tablespoons salt

2 tablespoons brown sugar

2 tablespoons paprika

2 tablespoons cumin

2 tablespoons coriander

1 tablespoon cayenne

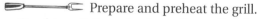 Prepare and preheat the grill.
   Combine all the spice ingredients. Brush steaks with olive oil then dredge them in the spices. Grill steaks over hot fire for 4 minutes per side for medium-rare.

Serves 4 to 6

GARLIC-OREGANO STRIP STEAKS

The oregano gives a nice Italian flare to these steaks. Serve freshly grated Parmesan or Romano cheese on the side, if you like.

4 Kansas City strip steaks, each 1 inch thick

2 cloves garlic, minced

1 tablespoon olive oil

1 tablespoon oregano

Mix garlic, oil, and oregano together and coat each steak on both sides with mixture. Place steaks in a glass baking dish, cover, and let marinate in the refrigerator for 2 hours.

Prepare and preheat the grill. Remove steaks from the refrigerator and place directly on the grill over a hot fire. Grill for about 7 minutes on each side for medium.

Serves 4

Sesame Sirloin

A nice thick sirloin steak is a great cut of meat to feed a crowd.

1 sirloin steak, 2 inches thick

SESAME MARINADE:

1/2 cup vegetable oil

1/2 cup soy sauce

1/4 cup lemon juice

2 teaspoons brown sugar

1 teaspoon black pepper

1 teaspoon garlic salt

Place steak in a sealable plastic bag. Combine the marinade ingredients and pour into the bag, close, and refrigerate several hours. Remove steak from the marinade. Pour marinade into a saucepan and bring to a boil to kill bacteria.

Prepare and preheat the grill. Grill sirloin over a hot fire for 12 to 15 minutes per side for a rare center and medium ends. Baste while cooking. Slice steak across the grain and serve.

Serves 4

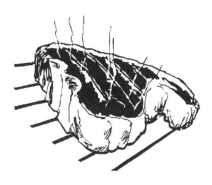

Fiesta Burgers for Four

When making any kind of filled burgers, form all the patties and make filling(s) the night before, but don't put the two together until right before you're ready to grill.

1½ pounds ground chuck

Garlic salt and freshly ground pepper

¼ cup chopped tomato

¼ cup chopped jalapeño pepper

¼ cup chopped fresh cilantro

¼ cup chopped scallion

Combine tomato, jalapeño, cilantro, and scallion and set aside. Divide meat into 8 equal parts. Flatten each portion into 8 patties. Place a fourth of the filling in the center of 4 of the patties to within 1/2 inch of the perimeter. Gently place a second patty on top of filled one, pressing edges together. Sprinkle garlic salt and pepper on each burger.

Prepare and preheat the grill. Grill patties over hot fire for 5 to 7 minutes per side.

Serves 4

Southwestern Grilled Beef Steaks with Three Pepper Rub

Serve these steaks with a garden fresh salsa of roughly chopped vegetables—tomatoes, peppers, onions, and freshly snipped herbs.

4 1-inch-thick beef fillet steaks

1 can whole green chiles

4 slices Monterey jack cheese

THREE PEPPER RUB:

1 tablespoon paprika

1 tablespoon seasoned black pepper

1 teaspoon white pepper

1 teaspoon ground red pepper

1 teaspoon brown sugar

1/2 teaspoon salt

1/2 teaspoon ground cumin

Slit a pocket in each steak. Place a piece of cheese in each green chile. Insert chile in each steak and secure with toothpicks. Combine rub ingredients. Spray steaks with olive oil and season with rub.

Prepare and preheat the grill. Grill steaks over medium hot coals for about 4 minutes per side for rare, or to desired doneness. Place steaks on indirect heat side of grill and cover with lid. Cook for an additional 2 minutes.

Serves 4

Steak Fromage

Try this recipe with thick chicken breasts or pork chops for a variation.

4 filets mignons, 6 ounces each

8 ounces blue cheese

4 slices bacon

1/2 cup (1 stick) butter

1/2 cup dry white wine

2 cups sliced fresh mushrooms

4 cloves garlic, minced

4 shallots, minced

4 tablespoons chopped fresh parsley

Salt and pepper to taste

Cut a slit in the side of each steak and stuff with blue cheese. Wrap a slice of bacon around each filet and secure with toothpick.

Combine butter, wine, mushrooms, garlic, shallots, and parsley in a sauté pan. Sauté over medium heat for 3 or 4 minutes until mushrooms are tender. Set aside. Prepare and preheat the grill. Grill steaks over a hot fire to desired degree of doneness and serve smothered in mushroom sauce.

Serves 4

Beef Tenderloin with Warm Balsamic Dressing

Convert this recipe into a vegetarian delight by substituting thick beefsteak tomatoes for the beef tenderloin and vegetable stock for the beef stock.

1 beef tenderloin, about 2 pounds

Salt and freshly ground pepper to taste

1½ tablespoons extra-virgin olive oil

3 shallots, peeled and minced

1½ cups beef stock

¼ cup balsamic vinegar

6 cups mesclun greens

Prepare and preheat the grill. Season the beef with salt and pepper. Grill over medium-hot fire for 10 to 15 minutes, turning every 2 to 3 minutes. Remove from grill and keep warm.

In a large sauté pan, heat the olive oil, add the shallots, and sauté for 2 minutes. Add the vinegar and beef stock. Cook over high heat until reduced by half. Arrange the greens on a serving platter. Slice the tenderloin and arrange over the greens. Spoon the warm sauce over the meat and greens. Season and serve immediately.

Serves 6

Greek Kofta Kabobs

Serve these tasty meatballs with a mixed green salad garnished with feta cheese and cured olives.

3/4 pound ground lamb

2/3 cup Italian seasoned bread crumbs

1/2 cup grated onion

2 cloves garlic, minced

11/2 tablespoons chopped fresh parsley

1/2 teaspoon ground cinnamon

1/4 teaspoon ground ginger

1 egg, beaten

Salt and pepper to taste

Combine all ingredients and blend well. Dampen hands and form mixture into 16 meatballs. Chill until firm, several hours or overnight.

Prepare and preheat the grill. Place meatballs in kabob baskets. Grill over a hot fire, turning baskets several times to brown the meatballs evenly. Grill 12 to 15 minutes or until meatballs are brown and crisp.

Serves 4

LAMB CHOPS WITH CHILES AND MINT

Roasted fennel potatoes and grilled baby green beans complete this meal.

8 lamb chops, 3/4 inch thick, about 6 ounces each

2 small cloves garlic, peeled and minced

Juice of 1/2 lemon

2 small hot chile peppers, minced

1/2 cup chopped fresh mint

 In a food processor, purée the garlic, lemon juice, chiles, and mint. Spread purée over lamb chops and marinate, refrigerated, for 30 minutes.

Prepare and preheat the grill. Grill chops over hot fire until browned on the outside but still pink on the inside, about 4 minutes per side.

Serves 4

Sage Grilled Veal Chops

Serve these tasty chops with "loaded" baked potatoes.

4 veal chops, ¾ inch thick, about 6 ounces each

Olive oil

16 fresh sage leaves

1 cup grapevine wood chips, water-soaked

Brush both sides of each chop with olive oil. Press 2 sage leaves on both sides of each chop and marinate, refrigerated, for 1 hour.

Prepare and preheat the grill. Grill chops over hot fire with moistened grapevine chips added, about 5 to 6 minutes per side.

Serves 4

Venison Chops

My husband Dick is a hunter and my first lessons in cooking were with game. I enjoy the luscious flavor of our Missouri and Kansas game that feed on the bounty of our farmers' crops. Occasionally, I'll hunt, too, enjoying the day in the fields with usually very little to show for it! Thank goodness Dick has better aim than I or the following recipes would not exist.

8 venison chops (deer or elk)

1/2 cup red wine

1/4 cup light soy sauce

1/4 cup honey

2 tablespoons chopped fresh basil

2 cloves garlic, minced

Place chops in a sealable plastic bag. Combine rest of the ingredients and pour into bag. Marinate chops in the refrigerator for 2 to 4 hours.

Prepare and preheat the grill. Grill chops over medium-hot coals for 4 to 6 minutes per side.

Serves 4

VENISON MEDALLIONS WITH GARLIC AND CAPERS

Wild game is very lean so it should be grilled over a hot fire quickly to avoid toughening the meat.

4 to 8 venison medallions or chops

2 tablespoons olive oil

2 cloves garlic, minced

1 tablespoon capers

3/4 cup white wine

2 tablespoons butter

Place venison in a sealable plastic bag. Combine olive oil, garlic, capers, and wine. Seal bag and marinate in the refrigerator for several hours.

Prepare and preheat the grill. Remove meat from marinade (reserving marinade). Grill meat over a hot fire for about 2 to 3 minutes per side, place on a platter, and keep warm. Pour reserved marinade into a sauté pan over high heat. When reduced by about half, add butter. Pour sauce over meat and serve hot.

Serves 4

Duck Breast with Red Raspberry BBQ Glaze

Duck breasts on the grill are best served medium-rare. Overcooking toughens the meat.

4 split duck breasts

1 to 2 tablespoons olive oil

Salt and pepper to taste

1 cup raspberry barbecue sauce

 Prepare and preheat the grill. Lightly coat duck breasts with oil and season with salt and pepper. Grill duck breasts over a hot fire for about 3 to 4 minutes per side, until lightly browned. Baste with the raspberry barbecue sauce and cook for another 2 minutes, then turn and repeat. Serve with additional sauce.

Serves 4

Charcoal-Grilled Quail

Apple, cherry, or grape wood chips added to the fire will complement this recipe.

8 quail, split

1 cup butter, melted

2 teaspoons fresh snipped tarragon

Salt and pepper to taste

Prepare and preheat the grill. In a medium shallow bowl, pour butter and add the tarragon. Dip the quail into the mixture and place them on the grill. Grill over a medium-hot fire for 3 to 4 minutes on each side. The quail breast meat will turn opaque and the underside will be pale pink.

Serves 4

Books on Grilling

The popularity of cookbooks available for grill enthusiasts is ever growing. Here is a list of favorites, some old and some new. For a complete list of titles on outdoor cooking visit www.pigoutpublications.com.

Appetizers on the Grill by Barbara Grunes
(1992, Chicago Review Press)

Barbecue Bible by Steven Raichlen
(1998, Workman Publishing)

Barbecue Inferno by Dave DeWitt
(2000, Ten Speed Press)

Great BBQ Sauce Book by Ardie Davis
(1999, Ten Speed Press)

Great Ribs Book by Hugh Carpenter and Teri Sandison
(1999, Ten Speed Press)

Grilling by Eric Treuille
(2000, DK Publishing)

Hooked on Fish on the Grill by Karen Adler
(1992, Pig Out Publications)

Hot Barbecue! by Hugh Carpenter and Teri Sandison
(1996, Ten Speed Press)

Grilling Encyclopedia by A. Cort Sinnes
  (1992, Atlantic Monthly Press)

Indian Grill by Smita Chandra
  (1999, Harper Collins)

Latin Flavors on the Grill by Douglas Rodriguez
  (2000, Ten Speed Press)

Pacific Grilling by Denis Kelly
  (2000, Sasquatch Books)

Que Queens–Easy Grilling & Simple Smoking
  by Karen Adler & Judith Fertig
  (1997, Pig Out Publications)

Thrill of the Grill by Chris Schlesinger and John Willoughby
  (1990, William Morrow)

Vegetables on the Grill by Shifra Stein
  (1998, Pig Out Publications)

Weber–Art of the Grill (1999, Chronicle Books)

Wild About Kansas City Barbecue by Rich Davis and Shifra Stein
  (2000, Pig Out Publications)

Wild About Texas Barbecue by John Bigey and Paris Permenter
  (2000, Pig Out Publications)

CONVERSIONS

LIQUID
1 tablespoon = 15 milliliters
$1/2$ cup = 4 fluid ounces = 125 milliliters
1 cup = 8 fluid ounces = 250 milliliters

DRY
$1/4$ cup = 4 tablespoons = 2 ounces = 60 grams
1 cup = $1/2$ pound = 8 ounces = 250 grams

FLOUR
$1/2$ cup = 60 grams
1 cup = 4 ounces = 125 grams

TEMPERATURE
400 degrees F = 200 degrees C = gas mark 6
375 degrees F = 190 degrees C = gas mark 5
350 degrees F = 175 degrees C = gas mark 4

MISCELLANEOUS
2 tablespoons butter = 1 ounce = 30 grams
1 inch = 2.5 centimeters
all purpose flour = plain flour
baking soda = bicarbonate of soda
brown sugar= demerara sugar
confectioners' sugar = icing sugar
heavy cream = double cream
molasses= black treacle
raisins = sultanas
rolled oats = oat flakes
semisweet chocolate = plain chocolate
sugar= caster sugar